Can't See the Wind

BUT THE EVIDENCE IS ALL AROUND

Practical Insights of God's Involvement in Everyday Life

Laurie Ganiere

Scripture taken from The Voice™. Copyright © 2008 by Ecclesia Bible Society. Used by permission. All rights reserved.

Scriptures taken from the Holy Bible, New International Version®, NIV®. Copyright © 1973, 1978, 1984, 2011 by Biblica, Inc.™ Used by permission of Zondervan. All rights reserved worldwide.

Scripture taken from The Message. Copyright © 1993, 1994, 1995, 1996, 2000, 2001, 2002. Used by permission of NavPress Publishing Group.

Scripture quotations marked (NLT) are taken from the Holy Bible, New Living Translation, copyright © 1996, 2004, 2007 by Tyndale House Foundation. Used by permission of Tyndale House Publishers, Inc., Carol Stream, IL 60188. All rights reserved

Scripture taken from the New King James Version®. Copyright © 1982 by Thomas Nelson, Inc. Used by permission. All rights reserved.

Cover Design: Sarah Dams

Cover Photo: Vicki Oseland

TABLE OF CONTENTS

DEDICATION

To the love of my life, next to Jesus, my very best friend and soul mate, Rick Ganiere. I love you and love the journey we travel together.

To my children, Cari, Christopher, Craig and Ricky:
You are more than a mother could ever hope and dream for. I'm so very proud of each of you and your families. Love you to the moon and back.

To those that have been encouraging me for many years to put my writing in a book – you know who you are. I love you and thank you for your prayer and encouragement.

To Vicki Oseland, an incredible photographer.
Thank you for allowing us to use your work in our cover design. Your photos captivate me!

To Sarah Dams, your skills confound me. Thank you for all your help in all the countless details of this work.
You're awesome!

To my God, My Savior, My Redeemer, My Friend.
I can't imagine my life without you. You ARE my everything.

FORWARD

Thank you for entering this journey in **"Can't See the Wind."** This work was well in process when I read a book on how to write a devotional. It was a great book, <u>"Write That Devotional Book: From Dream to Reality"</u> by Lee Warren. It had an immense amount of practical information. I am so very grateful for it. I saw some things that I already had done backwards. If you don't know me, that is really quite typical of many things in my life.

The author said that you should start with a title first. Well, the work was near done and I couldn't come up with a title. I thought I had one, but it just didn't feel right. Then, one Sunday morning, I was listening to my Pastor, **_Todd Pope of Waukesha First Assembly_**, sharing a part of his message series **"<u>Evidence.</u>"** He was talking about how even though we can't physically see God, we see evidence of Him all around us. He also said that the same thing is true of the wind. You can't see it, but the evidence of it is all around. BOOM! That's it!!! Can't See the Wind.

I see the evidence of the wind quite clearly. I can't see the wind, but I have a whole new hairdo when it's windy. I can't see the wind, but our leaves are in our neighbors yard because of the great wind that took them there. I can't see the wind, but I can hear the flags whipping on their posts next door. I can't see the wind, but it takes the sail boat moving along at a rapid speed.

In the same way, we can't see God, but the evidence of Him is everywhere around us.

I can't see Him, yet He reveals Himself to me every day in all kinds of ways. This devotional, or small group study, is full of every day experiences that help us to discover His involvement in everything in our lives.

My prayer for you is that as you journey through **Can't See the Wind**, that you are able to see God a little clearer in your own life. That He reveals to you His great love, mercy and grace in day-to-day things.

So, put on your jacket and tie down your hat. It's windy out there. How do I know? The evidence is all around. Be blessed friends.

Laurie Ganiere

∽⊙℮ | ℮⊙∾
But Then Jesus

There are so many inspiring stories of Jesus healing. To name one, the lame man at the pool of Bethesda, John chapter 5. For thirty-eight years he lay there, hoping to get into the water when it was "stirred", so that he could be healed. But he had no one to help him. But then Jesus! So many of us have had "but then Jesus" moments in our lives. Broken lives, but then Jesus. We love those stories. They increase our faith to continue to believe in the midst of life's difficult circumstances.

Like so many of us that have been touched by God, the guy picks up his mat and on his way he goes. Healthy and whole for the first time in thirty-eight years! But it doesn't end there. Continuing in John 5:14, *Later Jesus found him at the temple and said to him, "See, you are well again. Stop sinning or something worse may happen to you."* Jesus said very similar words to the woman that was caught in adultery in John chapter 8.

See here's the thing: an encounter with Jesus changes the way we live. At least it should. The choice is ours to walk in new life or to just keep going on the path we've always walked. God wants to pour blessing into our lives, but He won't bless a mess. If we choose to go back into our mess, His blessing won't be on us.

I've seen so many people over the years accept Jesus Christ as their Savior, but they never accept Him as Lord. They only give Him a part of them, kinda like sticking Jesus in their backpack of life. He's there when they need Him, but He doesn't live in their heart. They continue to make bad decisions, doing some of the same things they did before and wondering why God isn't blessing them. It's because the WHOSE we are isn't matching the HOW we live.

An encounter with Jesus changes us from the inside out. When we make Him LORD AND SAVIOR. Then He gives us His Word to show us how to live our life as an example to those in our sphere of influence of the life changing power of Jesus Christ. **Romans 12:2 (Message)** *"Don't become so well-adjusted to your culture that you fit into it without even thinking. Instead, fix your attention on God. You'll be changed from the inside out."*

He doesn't save us and heal us to make us feel better. He saves and heals us to make us holy. Our lives are an example to those in our sphere of influence of the life changing power of a living God. *So if you're living too close to the world, fitting in where you should be stickin' out, change that today.* The blessing in Deuteronomy 28 will be yours if you walk in obedience to Him. You'll be blessed in and out, when you come and go, in your work and in your home, you will be the head and not the tail... read it. It's awesome.

And think of those in your life who desperately need a "but then Jesus" experience! Begin praying for them today.

PERSONAL REFLECTIONS

- What areas of your life are you experiencing the blessing of God?

- What are the areas of your heart that you've kept from Him?

- Make a plan today to move Jesus from your backpack to having complete control of your heart.

- Then make the necessary changes to not go back. Remember, a plan is only as good as your ability to measure its success.

- Decide on three measurable changes that you will begin to make today to live a life in the power of His Spirit.

2
Life-Giving Well or Dark Cave of Abuse

Proverbs 10:11 NIV *"The mouth of the righteous is a fountain of life, but the mouth of the wicked conceals violence."*

Proverbs 10:11 from the Message reads: *"The mouth of a good person is a deep, life-giving well, but the mouth of the wicked is a dark cave of abuse."*

I am forever amazed at the number of scriptures that speak to the ability of our mouths to breathe life or death into another human being. And how often some ignore those words on a day-to-day basis is baffling to me. As Christians, we have to ingest and allow this truth and live by it: ***Words Matter! The tone and emotion of the words we use matters also to everyone in our sphere of influence.***

I wish I could tell you that this is a slam-dunk for me, but it's not. I wish I could tell you that I always speak with healthy tones and emotions in the words I use, but I can't. I'm not proud of that, but if I'm going to be real, I have to admit that there are times when I feel the sharp conviction of the Holy Spirit with the tone or emotion of a word. I don't often use bad words, but tone and emotion will bless or curse.

"A study was done by psychologist Dr. Henry H. Goddard, on energy levels in children. He used an instrument he called the 'ergograph.' (*An ergograph is an instrument that measures and records the work done by particular muscle groups.*) How he ever got some children to stand still long enough to connect them to the machine is a mystery. But he did, and his findings are fascinating. "He found that when tired children are given a word of praise or encouragement, the ergograph shows an immediate upward surge of new energy. When the children are criticized and discouraged, the ergograph shows their physical energy take a sudden nosedive." Holwick's Illustrations

This is fascinating. For those of you that enjoy physical proof of spiritual truths, this is a study to know the affect of our words. Words matter. The way we use those words matters. The scripture says they are a life-giving well or a dark cave of abuse. The choice is ours.

The old song we used to sing as kids, "Sticks and stones can break my bones, but words can never harm me." Lie from the pit of hell. Words matter.

You choose:
- Praise and encouragement = life-giving well = strength, surge of energy
- Criticism and discouragement = dark cave of abuse = depleted physical energy

Because some people were never spoken to with life-giving words, it's hard for them to naturally do it now. I promise you this – if you ask God to help you, He will! No question. There may be some of you that have people in your life that are just the "hard to be kind to" people. They're just mean. Ask God to help you breath life-giving words into them; that they could see that there truly is something other than the toxic dark cave of abuse that they may be living in. God will use you!!! I promise.

You get to choose how you invest in every relationship in your life. What will it be today?

PERSONAL REFLECTIONS

- What relationship(s) have you invested praise and encouragement into?

- What words of a "dark cave" have come out of your mouth?

- Ask God to forgive you for the criticism and discouragement that you have spoken.

- Asking forgiveness of those you invested criticism and discouragement may be in order. Ask God to show you and walk with you on that road to reconciliation.

- Is there someone in your life that could benefit from a gentle reminder of this scripture? Ask God to show you what part you may play in helping them see the life-giving well that is available to them.

✦ 3 ✦
Loving Those Around Us

Colossians 3:12-17 NIV *Therefore, as God's chosen people, holy and dearly loved, clothe yourselves with compassion, kindness, humility, gentleness and patience. 13 Bear with each other and forgive whatever grievances you may have against one another. Forgive as the Lord forgave you. 14 And over all these virtues put on love, which binds them all together in perfect unity. 15 Let the peace of Christ rule in your hearts, since as members of one body you were called to peace. And be thankful. 16 Let the word of Christ dwell in you richly as you teach and admonish one another with all wisdom, and as you sing psalms, hymns and spiritual songs with gratitude in your hearts to God. 17 And whatever you do, whether in word or deed, do it all in the name of the Lord Jesus, giving thanks to God the Father through him.*

I remember the night I received a call I had been dreading. My first Pastor, after accepting Christ in my life, Rev. Howard Lecher, had gone on to be with the Lord and his wife was in ICU in very serious condition.

The last time I saw him was an anniversary celebration for mutual friends, just a short time before that late night phone call. It was at that anniversary party that he called me off to the side and said, "Laurie, I need to talk to you. I want you to do my funeral." I could do nothing but hug his neck, and weep. Blubbering, my response was, "Pastor, I can't talk about this." Firmly he said, "We have to. I've told my children that I want you to do my funeral." I loved this man deeply as he was the first representation of Christ to me and was a true spiritual daddy to me. I still think of him so often as I hear particular scriptures, old hymns and often hearing someone just praise God openly, with a heart deep in love with their Savior.

As I read this scripture, I remember what the Word meant to him and how he taught me to cherish God's Word. So it is with that in mind, I share with you today...

- Be clothed with compassion, kindness, humility, gentleness and patience. Let others see those qualities in you every day. None of us is guaranteed tomorrow.
- Love each other, forgive as you have been forgiven – love people and walk in forgiveness as you have been forgiven. ***Unforgiveness corrodes the vessel that carries it.*** Forgive and it will set your heart free.
- Let Christ rule in your heart - we are called to peace. Who holds the reigns of your life?
- Let God's Word dwell in you - teach you and admonish one another with all wisdom - **LOVE THE WORD**.

- Sing psalms, hymns, spiritual songs - with gratitude in your hearts to Him. Don't be afraid to praise God all the time - in a crowd, alone in a room, everywhere you are, with the deep sincerity and conviction that touches the heart of God.
- Whatever you do, speaking or doing, do it in the name of the Lord - give thanks in everything!

One last memory of this precious man that I know I will see again - I remember as I was so new in the Lord, Pastor Lecher encouraged me to start a home Bible Study and invite my neighbors. My response was something like "Pastor, how can I do that, I don't know enough to teach a Bible Study." His answer was simple, "God will teach you as you reach out to your neighbors. You can do this, God will help you." Very prayerfully, knees knocking, teeth chattering and terrified, I began inviting neighbors. God taught me. Did I make mistakes? Did I say some stupid stuff? Yes. But God taught me. I learned early to crucify fear - *"God has not given us a spirit of fear, but of power, love, and a sound mind."* **2 Timothy 1:7**. I taught home Bible Studies for years, moving from one home to another, a whole new batch of people that needed Christ.

To you dear friends, crucify your fear – there are those in your sphere of influence that need to know that there's a God that loves them and has a plan for their lives. Allow God to use you with your friends, your neighbors, co-workers, and especially, your family. Love on them and let Christ shine through you. *Don't worry so much about saying the right things that you end up saying nothing at all.*

During the busyness of life, let the love of God shine through you today!

PERSONAL REFLECTIONS

- Which one of those six verses are the hardest for you?

- Unforgiveness keeps so many people spiritually bound. Release the pain of unforgiveness to the God that paid the price for it with His blood. Ask Him to forgive you, and to help you release them from the debt they owe you for all that was done.

- Loving others is impossible if unforgiveness has settled in your soul. Who do you need to forgive? Settle that with God today.

- Be free to love in Jesus name!

I recommend RT Kendall's book "Total Forgiveness". It will help you better understand what it is and what it is not.

4
The Gift That Keeps on Giving

A few years ago I had two surgeries back-to-back, one in November and one in January. Our biological family and our church family were absolutely incredible. Cards, letters, phone calls, gifts, meals and visits. My heart was overwhelmed by their expressions of love. The HUGE thing here was their love for God that compelled them to give to us. They each received a blessing from God when they gave. THEN.... my heart was broken before God. I was overwhelmed by the grace of God. There were many days lying in my bed, weeping at the goodness of God and simply saying "bless them God, bless them." That's why we say it's reciprocal. Both giver and receiver are blessed by that gift of love. I remember saying "God they didn't have to do this. They are busy people. They have jobs, families, responsibilities, but they chose to give to us. Because of their love for You, they give to our need. Bless them. Bless them. Bless them God."

2 Corinthians 9:6-15 Paul is talking about sowing and reaping. He's giving the church directives on the hows and whys. He says in verse 12 *"this service that you perform."* He's talking about the service of giving. Giving is a service? He said there are two sides to it: it supplies the needs of God's people AND it is our expression of thanks to God. That is precisely why earlier he says to make up your mind ahead of time, implying that it is to be thought through and purposefully done.

As I was meditating on this, I couldn't help but think about what motivates us to give.

- Sometimes we are compelled to give by the heartfelt need that is expressed, rather than emotional giving or that feeling of doing something noble.
- Other times, we feel pressured to give and our heart really isn't in it. Especially those times when they come around on your job asking for you to make the annual "give an hour's pay to some non-profit." We do it because everyone is and we would look stupid if we didn't. Even the "scrooge" gives to THAT.
- Then, there are the times when we know that God is putting something in our hearts to do. We see a need in a brother or sister and we make up our mind to do something.

That, Paul says, is a "service that you perform." You give to the needs of God's people AND it is your expression of thanks to God. Oh the excitement we feel when we are able to bless someone! What a gift to us to be participants with God on that, in that way.

Then in verse 14 it says *"And in their prayers for you their hearts will go out to you, because of the surpassing grace God has given you."* This is the reciprocal love that they express. **The gift that keeps on giving.**

That phrase, "the gift that keeps on giving" has been used about so many things. Giving blood, giving to non-profit organizations, and in a warped kind of way, giving premature "love away" with the reward of disease and loss of self-respect. But what the Word is saying here is that when we give, three things happen:

1. The needs of our brothers and sisters are met.
2. We release our praise and thanksgiving to God.
3. We in turn are blessed by our God.

There are many ways we can give to people. The obvious things we think about are financial, but giving to those in need is so much broader than that. Time, love, friendship, kindness, and on and on. You know what they are. Your heart is filled with the grace of God. Let that grace move you to give to those around you, whatever the need is. Give and you fill a need. Give and you release praise and thanksgiving to God. Give and it will come back around out of the hearts of those you touch through their thanksgiving to God for you. The gift keeps on giving.

PERSONAL REFLECTIONS

- What blessings have you been the benefactor of recently?

- In what ways has that encouraged you to pray blessing on them?

- Who is there in your life today that has a need that you know you have it in your power to meet?

- What sacrifice will you make right now, either in prayer, giving, or action, in thanks to God for all He has done for you?

5
Hee Haw

When I hear Hee Haw – I think of two things. The first is "It's a Wonderful Life", when the two old school buddies, George Bailey and Sam Wainwright, say "Hee Haw" to each other. Sam with thumbs in his ears, and at the end of a message at Christmas says: "Hee Haw and Merry Christmas." Sorry, some things just get stuck in your head. This would be one of them.

Hee Haw also reminds me of Balaam's donkey in Numbers 22. I know it doesn't say the donkey said "Hee Haw," but I'm thinking by the end of the story, Balaam wished it were just a Hee Haw.

Read Numbers 22.

God has given us a free will. He won't force us to do anything, including spending eternity with Him. He will, however, cause things to happen in our lives to get our attention. His plans are so much bigger than ours, and He just asks us to trust Him and follow Him.

Balaam inquired of God, but didn't do what God told Him to do. How often do we do that? Ask God and then not do what He says. When Balaam went his own way, God sent a messenger, an angel, to communicate that to him. He was so focused on other things, He never saw the angel. God used Balaam's faithful donkey to get his attention. The donkey, startled when he saw the heavenly messenger in the road, ran off the road into a field. Balaam just got ticked at the donkey and beat her, to get back on the road.

Again, the donkey knowing she couldn't pass that heavenly messenger, ran away from it, right into a wall. In the process of it all, it crushed Balaam's foot. Balaam became even angrier and once again beat the poor donkey. Finally, after seeing the angel again, the donkey, with Balaam on it's back, sat right down on the ground, refusing to go a step further. A third beating came.

Then the classic moment: out of the donkey's mouth came words, "What have I done to make you beat me three times?" Balaam said, "you made a fool out of me and if I had a sword I'd kill you right now." Again, the donkey speaks and says: "Aren't I the very same donkey you've always ridden? Have I ever been disloyal or hurt you?"

Wait – stop!!!! Didn't it occur to him that he was talking to a donkey? Seriously? I can almost hear somebody say: "I've talked to a donkey or two in my life." Not talking about THAT. Seriously though, Balaam was so caught up in the moment, stuck on being ticked at his own donkey, that he never realized that his own donkey, his trusted donkey, was **using words, not Hee Haws**?

The donkey says, "Am I not your own donkey, that you have ridden to this day? Have I ever done this to you?" **THEN**, finally, Balaam's eyes were open and he saw the Angel of the Lord. He had been so bound and determined to do what he felt in his own heart was right, that his pride and desires kept him from seeing God's messenger. Proverbs 14 and 16 tell us "there is a way that seems right unto man, but in the end it leads to death."

God will do whatever it takes to save His people. Even make a donkey talk if necessary. Though I think it would be very cool to hear a donkey talk, I wouldn't want God to have to go to such extremes to get MY attention!

So the word for us today is this: Walk or ride your donkey through life obeying the God that loves you. His plan is bigger and better than you could ever think. When you do, you'll never have to worry about angels with swords or talking donkeys. Hee Haw.....

PERSONAL REFLECTIONS

- Recount a time when God did something radical to get your attention.

- What did you learn from that encounter?

- Is there an angel or donkey in your life right now that you need to listen to?

- What will you do in response to God?

- What changes do you need to make to move forward?

∞◎ 6 ◎∞
What's New

Periodically, I ask myself this question: ***"Is there anything that consumes my time right now that I am better off without in the days and months to come?"*** Funny how God shows us what those things are if we really are prepared to let go of "that thing." Some of us may have gone through extremely difficult things in the recent past, and we must also ask the question: ***"What have I learned about myself, God or others that I need to take with me as I continue serving Him?"***

There's a line in the classic movie **<u>The Princess Bride</u>** where **Inigo Montoya**, played by Manny Patinkin, says ***"I've been in the revenge business for so long, now that it's over, I do not know what to do with the rest of my life."*** Seriously, one of the funniest quotes in the movie, but yet, also the saddest quote in that delightful movie!

Today Manny Patinkin says it took years before he realized the sadness and power in that statement. Some of us have been carrying around emotions, hurts, anger, bitterness, for so long, that we worry about what we'd do if we didn't have that safety blanket to hang on to. We've been unable to surrender them to God. Maybe yours or mine isn't revenge, maybe it's unforgiveness, maybe it's bitterness over something done years ago. Maybe it's a lack of trust, even well deserved. But if we ask God today what should be left behind, would He bring "that thing" to our minds?

Jesus said in **Matthew 6:14-15, "If you forgive those who sin against you, your heavenly Father will forgive you. [15] But if you refuse to forgive others, your Father will not forgive your sins."** As Christians, we're quick to say "I know that. I really do, but it's just so hard. If you only knew." Oh, but dear one, God knows. He told the Apostle Paul in **2 Corinthians 12:9 "My grace is all you need. My power works best in weakness."**

So in our weakness, we turn over "that thing" to the God that has the power to give us what we need to leave it behind. We participate with God in the work of forgiveness! Then, the next part of that quote from **The Princess Bride** – "I do not know what to do with the rest of my life," would read "I may not know what to do, but God in His grace will show me how to move forward without the ball and chain of that thing in my heart."

Maybe you are reading this and thinking, well, I really don't have anything that I have to leave behind. I would remind us all of the quote by **Dr. Martin Luther King Jr.** who said in one of his many riveting speeches, "He who is devoid of the power to forgive is devoid of the power to love. **There is some good in the worst of us and some evil in the best of us."**

So the question today - *"is there anything that consumed my time that is better left behind?"* God will show you and help you move on from that place. Regret is a huge emotion and energy sucker. Don't let it capture one more day of your life.

Or maybe your question is related to *"What have I learned about myself, God or others that I need to take with me into a better future?"* Identify what those things are and use them to invest in others.

As we wait for Jesus to return, invest with everything in you into people, the very heart of God.

PERSONAL REFLECTIONS

- Inspect your heart. Ask the hard questions.
  - What is in there that I would be better without?

  - Is there unforgiveness and or bitterness that I need to give to God?

- List some things that you have learned in the recent months, about God, about yourself, about others.

- How will you purposefully take those things into the next days, weeks and months and begin to invest in others?

7
Renewed Vision

I reread a story recently written by **Wayne Cordeiro**. You may very well have read it yourself. It reminds me of how different we view life and the affect it has on everything in our lives. The untitled story as written by Wayne Cordeiro: The story is told of two prisoners lying on their bunks one evening. The prisoner on the top bunk was staring out the window of his cell into the night sky. The stars were spread out in a splendid array, with an occasional shooting star making the evening sky a spectacular display of divine fireworks.

Calling to his cellmate in the bunk below, the man said, "Hey, wake up! Look at the stars! They're beautiful. Look!"

"Aw, leave me alone," his cellmate grunted.

"Come on. Just look. The stars tonight are the brightest I've ever seen."

His cellmate groaned and turned over in his bunk to look out at the night sky. After a brief glance, he growled, "I don't see any stars. All I see are bars."

One prisoner saw the stars; the other saw the bars. What we "see" is dependent on our attitude of life. You will either be a master or a victim, dependent on your attitude. The one cell mate was content in heart, thus he saw stars, not bars. Contentment is a heart issue.

There is so much sickness and heartache in the lives of those around us. There are so many that we see or talk to regularly that are so incredibly sick and have been for a very long time. Some are prisoners in their own bodies, yet they don't see their limitations, but continue to see God and all He is doing in and around them. Others are waiting on provision, God's provision, some for a very long time. They see the stars not the bars that would stop them. They continue to see the beauty around them and lament about very little, seeing the stars, not the bars. I am amazed at these incredible people. They are my heroes.

I wouldn't embarrass them and give their names, but they see stars, when no one would blame them for just seeing bars. Do you know what I mean? Who'd blame them, stuck in their situations, some for so very long. Yet, they refuse to give up or give in. They continue to trust God – and He helps them see the stars, not the bars. Oh they don't have their heads in the sand, they know their situations are grim. But their trust in God is bigger. Heroes. Heroes indeed! You may have them in your life too. In fact, if you don't, you yourself are probably seeing bars.

There are others that see only bars and there is no hope for anything in them. What a sad state to be in. A question I must ask is this: How can we say we believe in God and all He is and all His Word teaches us, and still only see bars? His Word is life, breath and health. It teaches us that He is in control of all things. All things are possible to them that believe. The way we see our lives makes all the difference in the world. We are either a master or a victim in our attitude? The Word teaches me how to live as a master of my own attitude. Heroes are masters.

My Mom was one of my heroes. She always saw the stars! There were times that I thought she was a Pollyanna, that she didn't really see truth, but had her head in the sand. I was so very wrong. She saw truth, and that truth was the fact that God had all things in His control. She was always able to see the stars.

So what do you see? Bars or stars? Listen to this: *Isaiah 40:25-26 NIV, "To whom will you compare me? Or who is my equal?" says the Holy One. "Lift your eyes and look to the heavens: Who created all these? He who brings out the starry host one by one, and calls them each by name. Because of his great power and mighty strength, not one of them is missing."* You dear one are of more value to God than the stars. Ask Him to help you see the stars. Then, lift your eyes and look.....

PERSONAL REFLECTIONS

- Is there an area in your life that you are seeing bars?

- List those bars by name. Ask God to reach down into your heart and change your vision – from the inside out.

- Start keeping a journal, every day, write the awesome things you see THROUGH the bars. Those stars!

- If you are the person that sees stars, ask God to give you the opportunity to pour into others to help them see the stars too.

- Pray for those bar seers in your life, that God would help them open their hearts to Him.

‿⁘〇 8 〇⁘‿
Let 'Em Search

In **Titus 2:1-8**, Paul is writing to one of his younger assistants - giving him instruction relative to church and the ministry. He gives specific instructions to every people group, older, younger, slaves, and free, and just basic instructions for how we are to live. So I can almost hear it now, "so it's gonna be one of THOSE devotionals. Telling me what I can and can't do." Well, as we saw in the previous devotion, it depends on your view on life. Do you want to see the stars or are you still bound by the bars. If you don't know what that means, read the devotion before this one.

One portion of scripture that stuck out to me especially was Titus 2:7 & 8 NIV, *"In everything set them an example by doing what is good. In your teaching show integrity, seriousness and soundness of speech that cannot be condemned, so that those who oppose you may be ashamed because they have nothing bad to say about us."*

As Christians, we live our lives in somewhat of a fishbowl. The higher the level of leadership, the bigger the glass on the fishbowl is. There have been times when I've been accused of things that I didn't do. Did I get mad? Absolutely! But I have to go back to what it says – that those that oppose us would be ashamed because there's nothing there. Does it really matter what they've made up in their minds about me? No. What matters is how I'm living my life.

We need to live a life of integrity. Integrity is defined as adherence to moral and ethical principles; soundness of moral character, honesty, with seriousness and sound speech that cannot be condemned. We need to ask ourselves this question: How do those that DO NOT claim to be Christians see us? Do they see us as people that are honest? Do they see us as people of integrity? As one of our sons says,"say what you mean and mean what you say."

Anyone that knows me, knows I'm not a legalist. I won't stand in judgment of others and make "scriptural judgments" on their lives. That's not my job. My job, if you will, is to make sure that MY life is showing people the right things, that I'm a Christ follower. So that when others see ME, they find nothing to condemn because there's nothing there. Paul says earlier in Titus that *"they claim to know God, but their actions deny him."* My job is to be sure that my actions SHOW Him, not deny Him. So, I say, let them look. Let them search!

Jesus lived His life with a lot of people continually trying to find something wrong with Him. What makes us think we are different? Get used to it. There have been a few times in my life that I've been accused of things that I had nothing to do with. No matter how I tried to defend myself, I couldn't. Those that accused me, didn't come to me, they went to other people. But if they HAD come to me, I would have had to "throw someone else under the bus," to vindicate myself. So I chose the high road, deciding that if they watched my life that close, they would see that my life is different than what they heard from someone else – gossip.

If we live with the kind of integrity that Paul speaks about, we would never bring shame to the cause of the Gospel. That's what we're really talking about here. It's not just about me and you, it's about the work of the Gospel. Are we afraid to have people look into our "fishbowl"? If we live a life of high moral character, we would have no reason to care. We would be honest in word and deed; men and women of integrity.

That's the challenge today - do you live a life that Jesus would be proud of? Do you live a life so integrity filled that even those that oppose you can't find anything there? Those that are looking for something to condemn you with can't find anything? There's nothing there to. I pray we do, you and I. Let 'em search. Nothing there but integrity and honesty!

God bless you friends~ Have a wonderful day in your fishbowl. ☺

PERSONAL REFLECTIONS

- When people look at your fishbowl, what do they see? Seriously now, don't get all self-righteous. To get a clear answer to that, measure your life with the Word.

- Ask God to help you see yourself clearly.

- In what ways do you need to clean your fishbowl, and what will you do today to start that process?

9
Crabs in a Bucket

Have you ever been around somebody that was a crab and you just wanted to get away from them? You reach the point where enough is enough, nothing you say makes a dimes bit of difference to them. They're crabby and quite happy right where they are. They want you to feel their pain - UNENDLESSLY. They grouse about everything – family's not right, church folks ain't right, bosses and co-workers don't act right. They'll often tell you they're really miserable, but have a bazillion excuses as to why they are the way they are. Just TRY to encourage that crab and you'll get bit too. They're just hard to be around.

The early church **wasn't** like that. If you read in Acts 4, particularly the last 6 verses, they took care of each other. Loved each other. Barnabas was even called the Son of Encouragement. Barnabas was the guy you wanted to be around. You always feel better about yourself and life when Barnabas is there. Oh, he wasn't the proverbial "Pollyanna" type who didn't see reality, he was full of encouragement that made you see things clearer and bring hope. In fact, you even aspire to be like him. If you're a crab, you don't much like being around a Barnabas type. You're happy sitting in your sorry mess.

Story has it that if you put a crab in a bucket, he will climb out without much difficulty. Without a secure lid, he'll break free of the bucket. If you put several crabs in a bucket however, they grab on to each other, pulling each other down, and nobody gets out. You don't even have to put a lid on the bucket because nobody's goin' anywhere.

So, if you're feeling a bit crabby, don't look for another crab, your mess won't get any better, and more than likely will get worse. Rather, find a Barnabas and he'll help you see through eyes that aren't bugging out like you're gonna have a stoke.

If you're a Barnabas, be careful. If God has called you to minister to those crabs, know when to hold 'em, and know when to fold 'em. Know when to walk away and know when to run. You need the wisdom and discernment that the Word brings. Stay in the Word, give the encouragement of the Word. Nothing else will help them escape the crab bucket.

Have an awesome day and stay away from the crab bucket.

PERSONAL REFLECTION

- What can you do when you start to feel like a crab in the bucket?

- If you're a Barnabas, glass is always half full person, begin to ask God for wisdom and discernment for the crabs in your life.

- If you don't have any in your life right now, hang on. Surely that will change. God doesn't tell us things for no reason. Surely you will encounter one or a bucket full of them. Ask God to fill you with the power of His Holy Spirit to make a difference.

- If you only help one from going into the bucket, rejoice in that.

⚜ 10 ⚜
Ty and David's Mighty Men

Read 1 Chronicles 11. It's the account of David's mighty men. It is very interesting and inspiring. Verses 22-25 tell of Benaiah, who went down into a pit with a lion on a snowy day. Mark Batterson wrote a book called just that, "In a Pit With a Lion on a Snowy Day." It's a GREAT book about risks and opportunities. When we take risks, we springboard into opportunity.

David and his mighty men fought - it included flesh and blood. It was about restoring God's kingdom, God's people, and God's honor. Our fight is most often, quite different.

Ephesians 6:12-18, 12 For our struggle is not against flesh and blood, but against the rulers, against the authorities, against the powers of this dark world and against the spiritual forces of evil in the heavenly realms. 13 Therefore put on the full armor of God, so that when the day of evil comes, you may be able to stand your ground, and after you have done everything, to stand. 14 Stand firm then, with the belt of truth buckled around your waist, with the breastplate of righteousness in place, ¹⁵ and with your feet fitted with the readiness that comes from the gospel of peace. ¹⁶ In addition to all this, take up the shield of faith, with which you can extinguish all the flaming arrows of the evil one. ¹⁷ Take the helmet of salvation and the sword of the Spirit, which is the word of God. ¹⁸ And pray in the Spirit on all occasions with all kinds of prayers and requests. With this in mind, be alert and always keep on praying for all the saints.

Our battle is a spiritual battle, not flesh and blood, but against evil forces in the heavenly realms. We are admonished to put on the full armor of God. We are to always be alert - always be prepared for battle.

With this thought, a picture of our grandson Tyler comes to mind. Ty is **ALL boy**. When he was little, just 4, he was always ready and watching for "bad guys." We were not sure what "bad guys" he was watching for, but the boy was ready. He wore his goggles, his Spiderman gloves, at times a cape, and always something in his hand taking the place of a weapon. He walked with a sway, hunched over, moving back and forth, always on the lookout, to protect his Mom, and everyone around him from the "bad guys." He was alert – he was ready. As he and Papa were on their way into McDonald's for dinner, he had all his gear on. When Papa told him to leave his "weapon" in the car, he said, "but what if I run into bad guys?" He was always ready, so why not in McDonald's too. So very cute and funny to watch his escapades of "getting the bad guys." The point is – he was always ready.

It challenges me to think about my own readiness. Do I have on the "full armor," ready to stand my ground? Do I have on the helmet of salvation and carry the sword of the Spirit, the Word of God? Do I pray in the Spirit? Have I allowed my armor to be sloppy with gaps and holes that arrows can get through?

I SO do not EVER want to run into a pit with a lion, not on a snowy day or any other for that matter. But I do know this, that if I have my shield of faith, the flaming arrows will only have the effect of cotton balls, extinguished and able to cause NO harm. So the question to us today is: Are we ready? If not, get your armor on - get the sword of the Spirit, pray in the Spirit. Take up the shield of faith. If you are ready: stand firm, always take steps to be alert. Get your praise on!

When we were with Ty, we always knew he was ready. How? Those goofy looking goggles, the cape, Spiderman gloves, his weapon in hand, and of course, the "walk." He was ready!

PERSONAL REFLECTION

- How have you experienced the power of God in times of difficulty?

- What are you facing today that you feel unprepared for?

- God will prove Himself faithful to you – you must apply the words of this scripture and get ready.

- What steps will you take to get ready?

- How will those in your life know that you are ready?

11
Seasons of Change

Ecclesiastics 3:1 NIV *"There is a time for everything, and a season for every activity under the heavens."*

From this point, the chapter goes on to talk about all the things that will change. I don' t know about you, but I am one that thrives on change. Some people break out in hives at the very thought of change, and people like me can make them very nervous.

When Rick and I were first married, he had no idea how much I thrived on change. In the home where he grew up, if a new piece of furniture was delivered, it stayed in that spot until the day it went to the dump. Except for cleaning of course. I, on the other hand, loved to move furniture around. Poor man had no idea! Late one night, after working a very long, hard shift, Rick walked in to a dark living room and fell over a table that clearly was not there when he left. His new, dear wife had moved the furniture around, showered and went to bed. I quickly learned to give him a heads up if I was moving anything.

Our lives go through seasons of change. Relationships go through seasons of change. It's really hard for those that hate change, or don't adjust well to it. For those like me, I come alive at the thought of change. It's a new season – time of creativity and new things.

One of the hard things for most of us is when relationships or friendships change, or cease to exist. We love people! We love the ministry that God brings to our lives as we invest in people. So that when any of those things change, it can be hard, even for those like me, to walk through that change and accept that it is a good thing.

It's hard seeing a friendship end. Even if it's for a good reason, there's a hole in our heart that is left vacant. If we can keep our eyes on Jesus and know that there is a season for everything, it is much easier to rejoice in that which was. Hold it dear in our hearts and thank Him for it. And, let it go. Move on with a thankful heart.

If we're involved in a ministry or a job, and the season for it is over, it can be a shattering thing. This too, we must be able to thank God for that which we had and be willing to look to the next thing. If we really believe that He has plans for us and that His plans are good, then get on it, that next float in the parade, and look forward to that season of change.

We live in a part of the USA where we have four distinct seasons. They come around every year – and I love each one. Whether I'm ready or not, that season is changing. I can grouse all I want that I have to put my motorcycle away until Spring, but I still have to put it away until Spring. I can drive my friends and loved ones nuts with my grousing. Or, I can move on with it, and know there are things I will miss in THIS season if I stay grousing about the last. Life changes friends. Thank God for that which was, and look forward to that which is yet to come. God is ALWAYS good.

PERSONAL REFLECTION

- Are you a person that enjoys change or dislikes change?

- What is changing around you and how are you dealing with that?

- Life changes – what do you need to turn over to God today and begin praising Him for those things that were?

- What do you need to do now to make the next changes easier?

‎12
There's Nothing New Under the Sun

Romans 16:17-20 NIV *"I urge you, brothers and sisters, to watch out for those who cause divisions and put obstacles in your way that are contrary to the teaching you have learned. Keep away from them. For such people are not serving our Lord Christ, but their own appetites. By smooth talk and flattery they deceive the minds of naive people. Everyone has heard about your obedience, so I am full of joy over you; but I want you to be wise about what is good, and innocent about what is evil. The God of peace will soon crush Satan under your feet. The grace of our Lord Jesus be with you."*

Paul was giving strong warning to the church in Rome. Stay away from those that cause divisions and put obstacles in their way. He was talking about others in the CHURCH that were doing this. They were more than likely "antinomians," being against the law, teaching that because salvation is grace, they didn't have to live in obedience to the law. They believed that a person could live in sin by rejecting God's moral law, and yet possess eternal salvation. They easily convinced people with their slick talk making their sin sound OK.

There is nothing new under the sun folks. We see this around us today. There are many who live their lives as Christians truly believing that their obedience to the law of Christ has no effect on them because they are SAVED by grace. They disregard the law – even that written in the New Testament, written TO the CHURCH. Jesus' teaching has everything to do with our daily lives and the choices we make. The grace of God isn't just a "big cover up." The grace of God gives us the ability to live a life of purity and holiness before our God. The grace of God is experienced through the power of His Holy Spirit IN us to live that life.

I see it often – those that don't make a connection between the things they do and the fact that they are Christians. They are blinded. As long as they can keep what they do separate from whose they are – they can live in sin and not feel conviction.

That's a scary, costly place to be. Our soul is at stake. Jesus paid a high price for your soul, and He speaks to us today just like He did in the days of old. Does our life reflect the one we serve, or have we just put our relationship with Jesus in a backpack for when we need Him? Then go on living our life the way we want to, our life not reflecting a life changed by Him? I'm not at all sorry if that offends anyone. The cost is too great for us to continue to live in sin.

Jesus told the woman that was caught in adultery to "Go and sin no more." After Jesus healed the man at the pool, He told Him to stop sinning or something worse would happen to him. Why? Because God's plan for us, the church, is that we affect change in our world, those in our sphere of influence. The grace of God has been slaughtered on many fronts by those that live in sin, yet claim to be Christians. Paul used strong words saying, "Keep away from them. For such people are NOT serving our Lord Christ, but their own appetites."

There's nothing new under the sun. The incredible, life-giving, freedom-giving, grace of God gives us the ability to live a life of obedience to Him in every area of our life. Paul said **"Be wise about what is good, and innocent about what is evil. The God of peace will soon crush Satan under your feet. The grace of our Lord Jesus be with you."**

There truly is nothing new under the sun. Be wise about what is good and innocent, about what is evil. If there are things in your life that you know are not pleasing to God, then stop it! Make a decision today. The cost is too great to continue on the path of indecision. He promises to give you what you need to do that. The grace of our Lord be with you.

PERSONAL REFLECTION

- How has your life changed since you came to Christ?

- How have you experienced His power in walking away from sin?

- If you have had Jesus in a backpack, keeping Him out of parts of your life, are you willing to make a decision today to take the steps of obedience and blessing?

Prayer: Father, forgive me for walking a different life than one that reflects You, my Savior. I am sorry for my sin (mention it by name). Forgive me I pray. I need you. Come into that area of my life and change me. Give me the power of your Spirit to walk away from it, and live a life that reflects your forgiveness, grace, mercy and love. Help me make that decision every day – to be the person You have made me to be. Help me to be a reflection of a life that others can see the "whose I am" matches the "what I do." In Jesus name. Amen!

13
That Little Voice

Psalm 141:3 (NIV), *Set a guard over my mouth, O LORD; keep watch over the door of my lip.*

My mouth needs a guard. Yes it does – it really does. Far too often my mouth gets ahead of my brain, leaving me in a quandary, wondering WHY in the world I said what I said. Have you ever been there? One would think that I'd get better at monitoring my mouth than I do. I mean really, how old am I? God knew what a big deal this would be for us – that's why there are so many scriptures that talk about monitoring our mouths.

The word "guard" in the original language means to protect or attend. So I ask God to protect or attend this mouth, and then don't give heed to Him when He does that. I can't imagine that I'm the only one with a mouth over brain issue. I can only imagine how frustrating I can become to my God who promises to do all that and so much more, and then He has to deal with my unwillingness to engage my brain before my mouth. He does His part, and I trample right over the little small voice that warns me, to protect me.

I have an orthopedic surgeon. I realize not everyone does, but this little pilgrim has one. I've gotten myself in more messes requiring orthopedic surgery. Some of them my own doing! I have a theory that if you were having fun when you broke it, at least there's some redeeming value in the break and healing process.

Anyway, Doctor Berry is a skilled surgeon, very kind and gentle man with a great sense of humor. After Doc replaced my left hip, he told me to forever be mindful of the fact that I have artificial parts. He was worried because I don't have a lot of sense at times, and think I can do most anything. Really, I'm the bionic woman. So I asked him when I would be able to get into the Jacuzzi. He said, "Before you ever do anything, I always want that little voice in the back of your head to say 'be careful'." He said the last thing he wants me to do is dislocate the new hip he "installed." Doesn't that sound lovely? Installed a hip? Anyway - his warning to me is to always have that caution in my head that says, "be careful."

My mouth needs the same caution. I need that little voice to warn me, to guard and protect the words I speak. The Holy Spirit is the "guard" that God gives us to protect or attend. We have a choice to either listen to the Holy Spirit or ignore the warnings. I can ignore that "be careful" warning that Doc Berry gave me. The warning was that I would experience more pain than I've ever experienced in life. So I don't ignore the "be careful."

If I don't heed the warning, the guard, the protection offered to me by the Holy Spirit, I will suffer the same consequences. I will bring pain into my life and those in my sphere of influence. So, I do my best to not ignore that small voice. Listen to that small voice. God help us to listen. Our ears are good, they work well, help us to listen and be blessed. Lord, help us to choose obedience to your small voice.

PERSONAL REFLECTION

- How have you experienced blessing from God when you listened to that "little voice?"

- How have you experienced pain or embarrassment for not listening to that warning?

- How can you better prepare for times of obedience to hear His voice?

- What do you need to commit to Him today that you have been ignoring?

14
My Way or the Highway

Proverbs 15:19, *The way of the sluggard is blocked with thorns, but the path of the upright is a highway.*

There aren't many things in life that are more frustrating to me than getting stuck in traffic. Come down I-43/894 any time between 4-6pm and you are subject to just sitting in traffic or moving at a turtles pace. I will do whatever I can to avoid that scenario. I will get off and zig zag through city streets to avoid traffic jams. Trust me, I am well aware that the time it takes me to zig zag through the streets may take as long, but I'm not STUCK in traffic - I'm moving!!!

I've heard others say things like, "I don't mind really. I spend my time in prayer or meditating." Forgive me please. I just don't get that. Oh, I understand praying and meditating on the Word, but THEN???? I feel like I need medication, not meditation. Get me outta here - I can't stay STUCK!

I remember being in labor and delivery with my first child and realizing that for the first time in my life I was in a situation that I couldn't get out of. There's only one way outta there. Talk about stuck. Before you feel like you need to "lay hands" on me, read the connection with the scripture.

The scripture says that a sluggard is someone that is habitually inactive or lazy. Another word in definition is "indolent" which means having a disposition to avoid exertion. They stay stuck on a path that is continually blocked with thorns. They can never get ahead and spend their time trying to find someone to bail them out of their mess. Their way is blocked with thorns - they get stuck at every turn in the road. They're sittin' in traffic, content to get nowhere fast. They may even be frustrated, but refuse to do anything about it, convinced their life is just one of thorns.

The second part of that scripture is about the upright. Upright meaning righteous, honest, and just. Our righteousness is in Christ Jesus, is it not? God sees us, His daughters and sons as pure, holy, just and in right standing. Our path, the path of the upright, is free of traffic jams. We don't get stuck - there is always a way through it. Don't misunderstand me - troubles come our way, yes they do. But we don't get stuck on the thorns, we fly through on a highway without traffic jams with the Holy Spirit guiding the way.

So then, the choice is ours. "My way" which is continually getting stuck on the thorns of life, or the "Highway," traveling the journey of life without traffic jams. The key is pursuit of God. For me, it's the Highway baby. Troubles may come, frustrations of daily life, but no traffic jams. We come through them without thorns.

PERSONAL REFLECTION

- Are you one who struggles with getting stuck?

- What are the "thorns" in your life that keep snagging you?

- What tricks does the enemy use to get you to look at the thorns rather than the path to freedom?

- Troubles will come. Pursuit of God is the key to traveling through them without jams. What steps will you take to pursue God today?

15
The Wait

Those of you that know me, know I'm not very patient in the "wait." It's just hard for me. This is very different than being stuck in traffic, like we talked about in the previous chapter. There are times that God has us wait, because there's a work He wants to do. It's never wasted time. It's a character building time. It's time to lay foundation. There's a work to be done, during the seeming "wait." That's true in every area of our lives, from family, to ministry, to work, to community.

We recently had a visit from a very good friend, Dave, who moved to Texas a few years ago. He was in town spending time with his dad following surgery. As we drank our coffee, Rick, Dave and I shared a lot. Mostly about what God is doing in our families and ministry. Our conversation took a zig zag as we talked about vision for the future. You know, those times when God gives us a glimpse of where He is moving in us or through us for the future.

I recounted the time a number of years ago that we were at a Missions Banquet. During that time in my ministry life, God had given me and my Board a glimpse of where we were going, and the work He called us to do. It seemed as though the fulfilling of that vision was simply taking too long and my patience was wearing thin. I was beginning to question whether I had misunderstood what God was saying. I was wondering if I missed the boat and was spending a lot of time on something that wasn't meant for me personally to do at all.

During that missions banquet dinner, a good friend asked Rick and I to take the missionary back to his hotel following the banquet. The hotel was very close to our home so we gladly accepted the opportunity to spend a few minutes with this great man of faith. We heard more stories of what God was doing in their country. He knew I was in inner city ministry, but that was all he knew. He knew nothing about my current struggles about the future.

As we pulled into the hotel driveway, we said our farewells, the missionary leaned forward, putting his hand on the back of my seat and said, "Laurie, though the vision tarry, wait for it."

WAIT, WHAT??? After he closed the door, I turned to Rick and said, "Did he just say what I think he said?" Of course he did. God used this man to confirm to me that He had given a vision, and that it was on the way. Wait for it.

So to you dear friends: if it tarries, wait for it. God is a God of order. He is working in you. He's working through you. He's setting all things in order for that time – because it will surely come. Though the vision tarry….. Wait for it. Waiting for a loved one to come to Christ? Waiting for the opportunity to begin walking in the vision He's given you? Waiting for that relationship to be restored? Waiting for……

Habakkuk 2:3 (KJV) *For the vision is yet for an appointed time, but at the end it shall speak, and not lie: though it tarry, wait for it; because it will surely come, it will not tarry.*

Habakkuk 2:3 (NLT) *If it seems slow in coming, wait patiently, for it will surely take place. It will not be delayed.*

Whatever your "wait" may be, job related, family issue, kids that have walked away from God, marriage, ministry, know that if God has given you a vision for it, it will come. Wait for it! As He works out the timing, He will not make you wait a minute longer than necessary. His timing is perfect.

PERSONAL REFLECTION

- In the past, how has God shown you that His timing is perfect?

- What is it that you are waiting for now?

- What has God promised to you about it?

- Knowing that God refines our character in the wait, how will you seek Him in this character refining?

❧ 16 ❧
Life Enhancers

Philippians 1:3-6 NIV *I thank my God every time I remember you. In all my prayers for all of you, I always pray with joy because of your partnership in the gospel from the first day until now, being confident of this, that he who began a good work in you will carry it on to completion until the day of Christ Jesus.*

Paul knew the power of an encouraging word. He knew that encouragement breathes life into people. God began a good work in you and He promises to carry it out until that great day of His return. He will never abandon us. Struggles in life sometimes leave us feeling like we just want to give up though, feeling alone on the journey.

Do you remember times in your life when others have spoken encouraging words to you? WOW, how it was a breath of fresh air! Those times when you felt like the "little train that couldn't" and someone came along side you to encourage you - "I know you can - I know you can" or "you can do it, come on, you can do it." Before long you were saying "I think I can, I think I can" and that turns in to "I know I can, I know I can." God sends those people to speak words into our lives that are like a fresh drink of cold water on a hot and steamy day. Those words give us what we need to continue and complete the work.

Before Rick and I began riding Harley Davidson Motorcycles, we rode bicycles. My husband, knowing his wimpy, outta shape wife's desire to just stay home instead of bicycling, was a hero to me. When traveling up a hill (or what he would say was a slight incline, trust me it was a hill), he would lag behind me. When I began to struggle, he would zoom up next to me, reach out and grab my bike, or my belt loops, and help me up the hill. What I dreaded became so much easier having him along side me. I wasn't sure how much fun it was for him. When I asked him about it, he'd just smile and say, "I just want to help."

Struggles are normal as we travel this journey of life. The question is, whom do you surround yourself with: Those that will breathe life or those that breathe destruction?

Walt Disney said, "There are three kinds of people in the world today."

- There are "well-poisoners." They discourage you and stomp on your creativity and tell you what you can't do.
- There are "lawn-mowers." People who are well-intentioned but self-absorbed; they tend to their own needs, mow their own lawns, and never leave their yards to help another person.

- There are "life-enhancers." People who reach out to enrich the lives of others, to lift them up and inspire them.

We need to be life-enhancers, and we need to surround ourselves with life-enhancers. Two questions to close:

1. Who do you surround yourself with?
    Well-poisoners? Self absorbed lawn-mowers?
    Life-enhancers?

2. Who are you? A well-poisoner?
    A self absorbed lawn-mower? A life-enhancer?

Invest in others as an enhancer. Make sure you have life-enhancers in your life too! God has begun a good work in you. He promises to complete it.

PERSONAL REFLECTION

- Thinking about yourself, not others, which of the three kinds of people are you?

- Ask a few others in your life, that you trust, how they see you. Sometimes we don't see ourselves as clearly as others.

- If they see you as anything other than a "life-enhancer," what steps can you take today to become that Godly encourager?

- Who do you see in your personal life that needs a "life-enhancer" to help them today?

৵৳ 17 ৡ৵

"Unda Da Sea"
Tombstone or Diver's Weight

Acts 24:1-27 Read this in your favorite translation.

We all go through trials. Some short, and some that seem to last forever. We've all been there. Your trial feels worse to you than mine – and mine feels worse to me than yours. We may have even sat around discussing those trials, trying to make sense out of them. Right? For the next couple minutes, I want us to look at the "during the trial." What's going on, really? And why? The longer the trial, the more we ask why. Some even get mad at God.

In the portion of scripture today, Paul was in prison, **again**. He was brought up on charges for everything from "I don't know what he's done" to "he's a trouble maker and stirring up riots." They passed him from one leader to another, leaving him in prison for a VERY long time, while they tried to make their charges stick. In Acts 16, there is the account of him and Silas being in prison and the great results of that imprisonment.

The main point is this: There's always a reason for every trial. There's always a reason for every seeming imprisonment in our life.

In chapter 24 of the book of Acts, Paul had conversations with Felix, an official in the Roman Empire, about righteousness, self-control, and the judgment to come. He used his time in captivity well and took every opportunity to speak God's Word. He didn't sit and wallow and complain. He used it as an opportunity. You see, *God will never release us from the trial until the purpose for it is accomplished.* Let me explain.

Someone once said that "the trials we go through can feel like a **tombstone** around our necks meant to destroy us, when really they are the **weight that holds the diver down** under water as he searches for pearls." The question in my heart today is "do we see our trials as a tombstone or a diver's weight?"

> God will never release us from the trial until the purpose for it is accomplished.

Our pessimistic under water goggles tell us certainly it's meant to destroy us. God's Word teaches over and over that trials come for purpose, especially for us to see the faithfulness of God. He will never leave us "unda da sea" so long that we won't have any air, but just long enough for us to gather all the pearls that are meant to be ours. We are forever learning - forever gathering pearls. You're trials aren't meant to destroy you. But they are opportunities to find some gorgeous pearls!

So do you see a tombstone or a diver's weight? If you're "unda da sea" in some area of your life, start looking for those pearls. "Unda da sea, unda da sea..." you know the rest. In case you are one of those rare people that have no connection to the phrase "unda da sea," YouTube it and you will find a great song from the Disney movie The Little Mermaid.

PERSONAL REFLECTION

- In trials, is it more natural for you to see tombstones or a diver's weight?

- In what ways in the past has God shown you incredible pearls while you were "unda da sea"?

- What is going on in your life that feels like a tombstone? You feel like you're going to drown.

- Ask God to defog your goggles. Tell Him you want to find the pearls. Make that decision today to start looking for those pearls. He will help you. I promise!

∾◌ 18 ◌∾
Child's Faith, Adult's Lesson

Read John 6:1-14 in your Bible.

This is such a precious account – 5,000 hungry people and no food to feed them. Then, a young boy with five barley loaves and two small fish gave Jesus his food. The adults struggled, they couldn't imagine how this was going to work. Can you imagine the boy watching his food multiply??? He learned that if he gave Jesus what he had, Jesus would multiply it to meet the need. Certainly a lesson we adults need to re-learn.

We struggle when we just don't know how the dollar is gonna stretch; when we know something is out of our control; those times when someone we love is sick and we don't have it in our power to do a stinkin' thing about it; when we don't have two nickels to rub together to make a dime. A few pennies maybe, but nickels?? This little guy learned that Jesus multiplied resources.

I have the most awesome grandchildren on this earth. I love them so much and enjoy hearing their take on God's involvement in their lives. One of my grandsons told his mother that he and God were riding in a car one day, and God brought him to their house and told him that she was the best Mommy- so God left him there for her. Not sure what Bible story he got that from.

Granddaughter Addy told a story about how Jesus turns water into root beer, and how Jesus was sleeping in a boat with the disciples and the storm came and they woke him up. Jesus got mad and threw all the guys outta the boat. Sorry Sunday School teacher, we know you didn't tell it that way.

One of the greatest stories she told was how she prayed for something impossible for her fish Lisa. I was sitting with her one day and the story went like this:
"Nana, my fish 'Weesa' died."

"Oh Addy, how sad," I said.

Addy continued, looking ever so sad,
"I cwied and I cwied."

With my sad Nana face on, I said,
"Oh Ad, I'm so, so sorry."

Then she perked up and said:
"Me and Momma pwayed and she comed back."

Picture it, me, Pastor Nana here, looking in shock at my daughter-in-law, saying something spiritually profound like: "Really?? Seriously?" Casey smiles and says, "Yup, look, she's swimmin' in the bowl behind you." She went on to tell me that "Weesa" was deader than dead, floating belly up and Addy was so sad. They prayed. God answered the prayer of that child.

I know I'm Nana, but come on, isn't that the greatest fish story you ever heard? I am so blessed to know that the same way that God taught that little boy with the loaves and fishes faith, He is teaching my kids and grand babes. If you are a Mom, a Dad, Sunday School teacher, Boys or Girls club teacher, know that you are making a difference. Keep investing in the kids. They won't ever be afraid to trust God with their fish and bread.

As adults, do we have that same childlike faith? God is a debtor to no one. God loves it when we come in faith and ask. *"So let us come boldly to the throne of our gracious God. There we will receive his mercy, and we will find grace to help us when we need it most."* **Hebrews 4:16**

PERSONAL REFLECTION

- Make a list of the times that you experienced God multiplying resources.

- During those times of need, what have you learned about God, yourself or others?

- Thank Him that He loves you and continues to show you His grace, mercy and love.

God wants us to ask – to come boldly. What do you need to come boldly to Him for today?

19
His Reflection

Some of you, like me, have seen the play **"The Lion King,"** or at least saw the Disney movie when it came out in 1994. Our oldest Granddaughter fell in love with the movie when it came out. She was just two then. She and I went to see the play a couple years ago. It was truly spectacular and a night to remember.
The story, the life of a lion cub, Simba, done with so much tenderness, drama, and humor that it was hard to remember that these people were portraying animals.

The most compelling part of the entire play was the last couple of scenes. Simba, was now grown, living in fear knowing his father, Mufasa, who he thought would be with him always, was gone. And to make it worse, Simba believed the lie that it was his fault! Who was next in line to rule? Simba! He could not, however, come to grips with his role without the strength of his father. He could not be King - not without Mufasa.

Hang with me just a second longer – as I'm sure you are wondering what this has to do with a devotion?

Act 2, scene 6 of the play: Simba is gazing into the water and sees not his own reflection, but his father's. The chorus of the song they sing is: "He lives in you... Have faith, he lives in you, he lives in me, He watches over... he lives in you..."

I was amazed at the deep emotion I felt and the connection with some truths in the Word of God. Don't misunderstand me - the Lion King is not a gospel message. However, grasp the deep understanding that He is alive in us – our God who lives in us, and it is His reflection we bear. The one whose power is in us because He lives in us!

As God's people, we reflect the image of our God. It's because of Him that we live, move and have our being. We are created to mirror His image to those in our sphere of influence.

As that young cub, Simba, lived in fear, knowing that in himself he could never measure up to the man his father was, many of you may be living in fear, feeling that you just can't measure up either. Simba didn't realize the power and authority that was his because of who his father was AND the fact that his father was IN him. Often times you and I forget the power and authority that is ours because of **Who our Father is and that His Spirit lives in us.**

Colossians 3:10 NIV, *"...put on the new self, which is being renewed in knowledge in the image of its Creator."* The word "image" means "likeness, representation." You reflect the image of your God. Because **He is IN YOU.**

You and I need to look, not in a pool to see a reflection of our God, but into the Word of God, to see who we are in Him. We are made to be a reflection of Him - His power and authority. *He lives in YOU.*

Romans 8:11 NLT *The Spirit of God, who raised Jesus from the dead, lives in you. And just as God raised Christ Jesus from the dead, he will give life to your mortal bodies by this same Spirit living within you.*

No matter what comes into your life, know THIS truth! **HE LIVES IN YOU!!!**

PERSONAL REFLECTION

- How can you relate with the character of Simba, experiencing some fear that God is not here physically?

- In what ways do you want God's reflection to be seen in you?

- How does it make you feel knowing that you bear God's image?

- In what area of your life do you struggle with the lack of God's reflection?

- Have that conversation with God now, turning it over to Him, that you would bear His image to those in your life.

❧ 20 ☙
La La La La

Read John 6:60-71 in your Bible.

Do you remember as a kid, covering your ears and singing "la la la" trying to drown out something you didn't want to hear? I knew as a kid that if I did that, nothing good was going to come of it. Now as adults, we do it jokingly, making our feelings known in a jovial sort of way. But none-the-less, getting our point across that there's something we don't want to hear.

Jesus had just finished the wonderful teaching about the bread of life, one that many of us know well. There was a wide variety of people there, some that found his teaching simply too hard to listen to. Many said: "This is hard teaching, who can accept it?" Verse 66 says: *"From this time many of His disciples turned back and no longer followed Him."*

What? They were His disciples and turned back?? No longer followed Him? They heard something that was too hard to hear so they left Him. By walking away, they showed how they were covering their ears, singing as they went away. Singing about how harsh something is. Singing about how unfair it is. Singing about how there's no way they will do what He asks. Singing about how it just doesn't make sense. Singing about how…. You name it!

How do I know that? Because it still happens today. We hear something we don't like - we lack understanding, or just plain don't like it or what it requires of us, so we go "MIA," missing in action. The same choice as the deserters made all those years ago, many make the same decision today. All because we don't like what is said, or find it just too hard to wrap our heads and will around it.

Jesus turned to the twelve and asked them if they were going to leave too. Peter's response was classic: "Lord, to whom shall we go? You have the words of eternal life. We believe and know that you are the Holy One of God." He basically said they burned their bridges. There is nothing back there for them. They found Him, the Holy One of God, there's nothing to go back to.

When it gets tough, don't cover your ears and sing that stupid "LA LA LA" song. When the road gets hard, don't walk away. Kids do that and then wonder where they're going to go. Where are you going to go? You could be missing the teaching of your life, all because it's hard and you've chosen to cover your ears. Or maybe it was hard and required more than you were willing to give.

Has He interrupted your day with something you just don't want to deal with? Listen - it could change the rest of your life. Don't ignore it - press in. He will make it clear if you will just not walk away. Burn those bridges, hang tough, and recognize that as Peter said "You have the words of eternal life. We believe that YOU are the Holy One of God." Make a decision today to never cover you ears. Live, learn, walk in obedience, walk in victory, walk in His blessing. He IS the Holy One and has great plans for you my friends! Have a victorious day!

PERSONAL REFLECTION

- Recall a time that you covered your ears to what God was telling you.

- What happened when you made the decision to actually listen?

- Is there an area of your life that you've been ignoring God's voice?

- How will you unplug your ears and walk that journey toward grace, mercy and blessing?

⚘❧ 21 ❧⚘
Starbucks At Lunch

I stopped at Starbucks the other day to get a yummy Dulce de Leche. While en route, I was listening to one of the local "talk radio" stations and a conversation about fashion faux pas. One guy said: "Just because they make it in your size doesn't mean you should wear it." Well, we all can get a picture of what THAT means. The majority of us don't have a body shape that is perfect. I would hope that most of us have the good sense to put on things that fit right. And hopefully, we know the difference between what should be worn in the privacy of our home and what can be worn in public.

With summer approaching in the Midwest, it's the season that we see all kinds of folks that put on things that are only fit to be worn in the privacy of their own homes. Sadly, many don't see themselves through the same lens that others do. We don't see ourselves truthfully.

On the other hand, some that have worked hard to be "fit," always see their flaws when the rest of the world sees very fit and in shape bodies. It's like the rest of us that see ourselves looking good in many things that are best left to those who are fit. Like the guy on talk radio said "just because they make it in your size doesn't mean you should wear it."

The same guy that made the comment about the size thing said to the men: "Guys if you don't have muscles, don't wear a muscle shirt."

Wait! What IS the point of this devotion? Well, we as human beings have this uncanny ability to measure ourselves by ourselves rather than measuring ourselves against truth.

We measure ourselves by what we WANT to be rather than what we really are. We make messes, cause ourselves embarrassment, shame and occasionally even get ticked at God because of the reproach it brings. Sometimes, it also brings great reproach to the Body of Christ, because we keep measuring ourselves by ourselves. **2 Corinthians 10:12 NIV,** *"When they measure themselves by themselves and compare themselves with themselves, they are not wise."*

Proverbs 19:3 NLT, *"People ruin their lives by their own foolishness and then are angry at the LORD."* Our own foolishness makes a mess and we get ticked at God. It's really uncanny how we do that.

Make decisions, today and every day, based on truth not the lens of this world, or your own sinful lens of life. The truth, the only truth, is found in the Word of God. Let God guide your day-to-day decisions, even about dress. The Word of God will never bring you OR God shame, embarrassment or reproach. See yourself through the goggles of truth - the Word of God.

A side note: I called my daughter right after hearing this show on the radio and made her promise me that if I ever wear anything that was way too "young" for me or this outta shape body, that she would tell me. She said, "Yes, I will - if you promise not to yell at me." We both had a good laugh. Measure yourself with the Word of God. And if someone you love tells you something is wrong, pay attention.

PERSONAL REFLECTION

- How have you personally experienced some clouded vision about yourself?

- What did you discover God's Word had to say about that?

- Are you seeing things clearly now, or is there something you're not sure about?

- How and where will you seek to find that truth?

- Will you take the risk of allowing truth tellers in your life?

22
Easier Than You Think

As I was meditating on obedience today, I see that it's easier than we think to be deceived by our own good works. How so? Well, we think that if we're involved in good things that we are walking in obedience to Him. And to a degree, that can be true. But I also know that there have been times in my life when I've known that God has told me to do one thing and I do something else that seems so noble and right, thinking I'll get to the other thing later. Still doing a very good thing, but not THE thing that God told me specifically to do.

I was reminded of a story I read a while ago: One day a Dad and Mom had to leave the house to run some errands. The Dad said to his son, "Son, while your mother and I are gone, please get your room cleaned. Pick up everything and put it away, make your bed and run the vacuum." Sounds pretty detailed, not much room for misunderstanding right?

Son says, "OK Dad, no prob." A couple hours later the Dad and Mom return and the son meets them in the driveway all excited, big smile on his face, "Hey Dad,

Hey Mom." They all walk in to the house and everything looks awesome. The Dad says, "so what did you get done while I was gone?" The son, pretty proud of himself said, "Well Dad, I cleaned up the dishes and put them away. Then I cleaned up the living room and vacuumed. Then I even went into the bathroom and cleaned the tub after I took a bath." The Dad says, "but did you clean your room like I asked?" "Naw," said the son, "I'll get to that later."

The Dad was not pleased. Even though all the things the son did were great, they were not the things the Dad asked of him. **It's easier than we think** to do that which seems right and not do THE right thing. Are you living in obedience by doing what He has asked of you, or are you just busy doing stuff that seems right in your own eyes, and leaving the other things until later? **It's easier than you think** to get caught in that cycle. There have been times in my life that I did that very thing. I wonder, can you see yourself in that place too?

The Apostle Paul says in 2 Corinthians 10:12 *"...when they measure themselves by themselves and compare themselves with themselves, they are not wise."* How easy it is to do what we think is right and completely walk in disobedience to Him, even while doing good. We willy nilly walk through seasons of life doing good things, but not THE specific things He has told us to do. Seriously, **it's easier than you think.** The little boy did wonderful things. Who wouldn't like to come home to a house that is all cleaned up? But the boy missed it. Even though the things he did were awesome, it was not what his Dad asked of him. I'm sure he was very disappointed that his Dad was not pleased. I'm also pretty sure this was a great teaching moment for the Dad and his son. The spiritual application is huge.

Isaiah 1:19 NIV, *"If you are willing and obedient, you will eat the best from the land."* God wants to bless us. He wants us to prosper and eat from "the best of the land." That too **is easier than you think!** If you see yourself in this devotion, especially as the busy one doing all kinds of things, and not focusing on that specific thing, you must know this: **It truly is easier than you think** to come back to God and do what He has asked. He longs to bless you from the best of the land. *It's easier than you think.*

PERSONAL REFLECTION

- What is it about obedience that makes it so hard at times?

- What feeling do you get when you know you did something other than what you were asked or told?

- In looking at your life honestly, what do you need to do in order to "eat from the best of the land."

- How will you take steps today to begin walking in the favor of God?

I promise…

It's easier than you think!

23
Vineyard Pay

Read Matthew 1:1-16 in your Bible.

Recently, we had the pleasure of attending a presentation at one of the local churches. It had a strange title. Now, I'm not gonna lie, the title startled me when I saw it on Facebook. I wondered what it could possibly be about. As it turned out, it was a musical adaptation of God reaching out to man – all done in song, and a small amount of drama. It was well done and fun to watch, and participate in worship with them.

After it was all over, I talked to several that were in the production to tell them "Thank you for your ministry tonight." I always feel it's important to let cast, vocalists, and crew know that there are those, like me, who realize they could be doing any number of things instead of giving countless hours of memorization, rehearsals, and prayer into a production. They choose to give of themselves for the work of the ministry. Said all to say that I went up to a young man who had been taking care of the props. He also had a small part in the last song, sitting in a chair, portraying one that God was after. This precious young man, when I thanked him for his ministry, said "all I did was sit in a chair." I quickly reminded him that he was also in charge of moving props on and off the stage, and that everything he did was ministry.

My heart was grabbed by the tenderness of this young man. He didn't think he was "all that," instead he said "all I did was sit in a chair." My prayer would be that he would see the value he had to the King of Kings, the one that will give him his reward one day.

I also discovered that one of the dear ladies had just become a part of that choir just 2 practices before the performance. She did an awesome job, and entered into worship as if she was sitting in the pew. It was precious to watch and encouraged others in the audience to enter into worship as well, as did the rest of the choir. It was truly a worship time led by "the Church."

Looking at that event in light of Matthew 20, the story of the vineyard and the workers, I am reminded that none of us is more important or worth more than anyone else. Jesus told this parable to show us that no matter what we do for the kingdom, or how long we have done it matters to God. In fact, He said, "those who are last now will be first then, and those who are first will be last."

The young man who moved props on and off the platform was as much value as the man who wrote the script and the others that sang in that choir, or did special songs. We are all on the same playing field. In God's economy, that field is level.

So, no matter what you do for God, no matter how long you have been doing it, you are of value to God. Your wages in God's economy are all the same. No one is more important than another.

PERSONAL REFLECTION

- Are there times that you have felt like "all I did was sit in a chair?"

- What were you doing?

- Take a couple minutes right now and thank God for the opportunity He gave you to invest in the Kingdom.

- If you're seriously not doing anything to use your gifts or abilities for God, what can you do today to begin doing so?

ᏬᎣᏋ 24 ᏋᏬᏬ
The Energy in Synergy

Synergy - the interaction of two or more agents or forces so that their combined effect is greater than the sum of their individual effects.

It is so very inspiring to be a part of a work when you actually see this principle in operation.

For years, this was a very difficult concept for me to grasp. I see a lot of people today that have trouble with the synergy concept as well. Those who especially struggle with it often have control issues. "It" has to be done their way if it's going to be right, or they drive others nuts that are trying to work with them.

Others are last minute people, leaving it impossible to take the time to include anyone else in a process. They live constantly in the "tyranny of the urgent."

Yet others have serious pride issues and will share success with no one. Another face of pride is self-sufficiency. "We don't need no stinkin' help." It just takes too much time to include anyone else, they can get it done quicker by themselves.

I remember when my children were young, I was not the champion Mom when it came to my kitchen. All four of my kids can cook, some are VERY good cooks. I wish I could tell you that it was because of me. But truth be known, I had issues. I really <u>wanted</u> to teach them how to do stuff, but the urgency of the immediate would take over and it was just quicker to do it myself. You know what I mean? Timing is everything in the kitchen. Listen to me make excuses about how I would push them out of the way and just do it myself.

As a parent, or in the workplace or ministry life, sometimes it just takes too much time to explain how to do something. We think we actually save time if we just do it ourselves. Truth is, so much more could be done, if we learned the energy of synergy.

In the Old Testament, Exodus 18, Moses' father-in-law, Jethro, gave him some great advice. It was so good that the same principles are used in Church leadership and business growth today. There comes a time when every leader realizes that they just can't do the work alone. We have to find those to come along side and share the burdens, actually multiplying the affects of that work.

The Apostles learned that same principle in Acts 6. It takes an investment in people. When we invest ourselves in people, synergy takes over and the work accomplished is greater than the sum of what each individual could manage individually. This principle works in our homes, churches, work places and anywhere where there is any work to be done.

No matter who you are, you should be investing in people. No excuses. No matter how small or large your work or ministry, the key to success is empowering people.

I remember being the director of a huge outreach event that our church did. There were well over 200 volunteers and 2,000 attendees at this event. The event itself was only 4 hours long. The prep work began weeks before, and clean up was done within an hour of the event.

I remember people coming to me after and applauding me, throwing me kudos for making this event happen. My standard answer was this: there is no way I did this. The hundreds of volunteers working together set the stage for this to happen. We all locked arms for the glory of God.

So no matter who you are, parent, neighbor, ministry leader or volunteer, or in the workplace, the principle of synergy makes it possible to get more done through combined efforts. Feel the incredible joy in locking arms together. Watch the Energy of Synergy unfold before you, all for the glory of God.

PERSONAL REFLECTION

- How have you seen the energy in synergy?

- Do you find it easier to work alone?

- The next project you have, how can you include others?

- **Side Note:** It takes a certain amount of social intelligence to bring others along to work as part of a team. Be prayerful, asking God for wisdom. Then trust Him.

- If you've never been a part of a team, look for ways to volunteer your time and energies and see the power of synergy work. Each individual doing their part creates the energy in synergy!

25
The Lord Is Great

Isaiah 55:8 NIV *"For my thoughts are not your thoughts, neither are your ways my ways," declares the Lord.*

Psalm 40:16 NIV *But may all who seek you rejoice and be glad in you; may those who long for your saving help always say, "The Lord is great!"*

There is hardly a day that goes by that I, at some point, don't stop and purposefully say, "God is good." No matter what goes on in our life, He promises to meet every need we have, if we will seek Him, and trust Him.

During times of prosperity it is easy to say the Lord is Great. However in times of struggle or trial, it's not quite as easy. We often say, with great hesitancy, a "well I hope so," as if to put a question mark at the end of that statement. You know what I mean? The kind of hope that is questioning, not really sure that it will be ok!

We really want to trust that it will be OK. The key to those times of question, or worry, is to dig deep into our belief system. At the core of our belief and trust in Him must be that **He IS** who the Word tells us. **He IS** what He has shown us. **He IS** all that He promises in the Holy Spirit that dwells IN us. When we forsake the fear and worry and dig deep into that belief system, we come out with the courage to walk in complete trust that **He IS** good and that **He WILL** walk us through.

I remember when I was about to give birth to our 4th and last child. Dear Dr. Jacobson was certain that it was not safe for our child to be born naturally, and scheduled a C-section. After praying, Rick and I felt complete peace with this decision, knowing it was God's path for us and our child. While laying in Labor and Delivery, a friend from our church came bounding in the door and boldly insisted that she heard from God and that it was NOT God's will for me to have a C-section. She proceeded to pray against the "lies" that were told us and that this child would be born healthy and whole, naturally. No C-section. With that, she left as quickly as she had come.

My husband, dear sweet man that he is, knelt down next to the bed and began to pray. He asked God for wisdom in this decision, and that we wanted everything that God had for us and our child. With that, we both felt confident that we were to move forward with Dr. Jacobson's recommendation.

After delivery, the good Doc told us that had we delivered our son naturally, he would have had a severe neck injury. At the time of this writing, that child is 34 years old, healthy and strong. The scripture says "may those who long for your saving help always say, 'The Lord is great!'" We indeed said, the Lord is great as we squeezed that 9½ lb. bundle we named Richard Carl Jr.

Fast-forward a number of years, date, 2006 to be exact. I had necrosis in my leg, causing my hipbone to erode. Collapse of that bone made it impossible and dangerous to walk on it. After months of miss diagnosis, surgery was scheduled. Following a Sunday night service, there were about 20-25 precious saints that had gathered around me, praying the healing power of Jesus into that destroyed hip. While my dear friends were praying and believing, I was having a conversation with my Savior. See, He had already given me peace about the surgery that was to come. So I said, "Lord, I fear for my friends. I fear for the possible crisis of faith in them if they don't see a miraculous healing." God spoke clearly to me that night. "Laurie, they NEED to **see me** walk you through this. Let me worry about their faith." To which I said, "OK Lord, then let's go." Again, **the Lord IS Great.**

This is not a devotion about physical healing. I am a Pentecostal believer. I believe firmly that God does heal, miraculously heal, and often times, immediately. I also believe that there are other times healing comes over the course of time. Think about the man at the pool – 38 years an invalid. There are other times that God walks people through struggles and trials, so that they CAN declare that **"The Lord is GREAT."**

I heard a testimony of a man, a persecuted Christian in another country, right before a beating occurred, felt the kiss of the Lord, right on his ear, with a soft whisper from Jesus that He is with him and will protect him. That man had numerous beatings, and scars to prove them. Each time, Jesus was right there, with a kiss on his cheek, dew of heaven in a whisper of reassurance from Jesus Himself. Part of his testimony was that even

though we could see the scars, he never felt a one.
"The Lord Is Great."

This devotion is about how God will walk us through. It is about how in His great wisdom He knows what you and those in your life need. Because of that, we trust Him. **The Lord is great!**

Put your trust in Him. Sometimes it doesn't make sense. But trust Him anyway. His ways are not your ways, nor His thoughts your thoughts. May those who long for His saving help always say **"THE LORD IS GREAT."**

PERSONAL REFLECTION

- In what ways has God shown you that He is GREAT?

- Are you struggling with something right now that doesn't make sense?

- What steps will you take to trust Him in this journey?

- I promise you – He IS great.

Psalms 40:16
But may all who seek you rejoice and be glad in you; may those who long for your saving help always say, "The Lord is great!"

26
Get the Jars

Read 2 Kings 4:1-7 in your Bible.

When things don't go the way we thought they would, there is a principle we must hang on to.

This is a Godly principle, meaning you can't change it. **Blessing FROM God follows obedience TO God.**

The wife of a prophet came to Elisha some time after her husband died. She told him how her husband's creditors were coming after her and wanted to take their sons as slaves in payment of the debt. I can't even imagine the stress this caused her. She just lost her husband, and now they wanted to take her sons too? It was not her debt, it was inherited debt that she was left with. Now it might cost her the life of her sons. I can't even imagine the agony this caused her. How could this possibly be?

> Blessing FROM God follows obedience TO God.

In today's society, we'd scream "it isn't fair – I'm getting stuck with a debt that I didn't create. I'll have to file bankruptcy. Somebody get me outta this mess." And somebody would get us out of this mess. Our debtors would be left with the debt and we'd be free. Simply file bankruptcy. That's an option today. This devotion is not intended to heap guilt on those that have chosen the path of bankruptcy, but rather to show you an incredible principle.

Elisha let her in on a Godly principal. **Blessing follows obedience.** He asked her what she had in her house. Her reply was simply: "Your servant has nothing there at all, except a little oil." Elisha tells her to gather empty jars. Go around to all your neighbors and get empty jars. Then pour the oil you have – the LITTLE OIL you have, into the jars.

Some of you right now are saying, well that doesn't make any sense. It was only a little oil, in a little jar. **Only in GOD'S economy does a little become a lot!** When she was obedient, something incredible happened. Even when it made no sense! She and her sons began gathering jars, their jars and jars from their neighbors. Then they began filling the jars – from their "little oil jar." After filling every last jar, with that little bit of oil, the oil in the original jar went dry. He then told her to go sell the oil and pay off the debts. There would be enough for her and her sons to live on with what was left after those debts were paid.

The miracle was within her reach. As she followed the word that came through the prophet, she had enough to fill the need. She listened. She did what she was told to do. There was a miracle in the house.

Many of us fret so much and just don't stop long enough to listen to what God would say. We want the blessing of God but won't do everything necessary to reach it. We just want someone to give us what we need so that our situation changes.

God doesn't often just drop blessings in our lap. He didn't create us to be lazy people just to sit under a tree and wait for Him to solve every problem. More often He invites us to join Him in the process of meeting the need. It's what Dr. David Jeremiah calls the "Divine Cooperative." 100% us and 100% God.

We had friends over the other night that told us their financial need story. They were six figures in debt. They met with multiple financial people and bankruptcy attorneys. After all was said and done, they knew God told them to "work it off." I mean this was HUGE debt with nothing to start with but a "little oil," just like the woman.

God opened doors for them, supernaturally, and today, they are close to debt free. God has continued to bless them as they locked arms, in this "divine cooperative" with their God.

Your miracle may very well be just within your reach. Be it a financial, spiritual, physical, relational, or emotional. Maybe you need to start gathering jars, whatever those may be in your life. God wants you to partner with Him.

So go to Him. Ask Him for help, and then do what He says. He wants to meet your need but asks you to join Him as part of the process. Whatever it is, do it. God will include you in the process - you don't get to just sit and fret, complain to friends about how God isn't answering your prayer. Oh, don't get me wrong, you can do that, but you'll stay stuck. You probably have jars of some sort to gather. So get going!

PERSONAL REFLECTION

- How have you partnered with God in the past and seen His blessing in your life?

- What are you facing now that you really need "a miracle in the house?"

- Have you asked God to show you what to do?

- If He has, then get going and do it. If he hasn't, what steps can you take to partner with Him?

100% God and 100% You
=
Miracle in the House

27
He Keeps Watch Over You

I'm just so glad that God never leaves us. He is always there, always in protector mode. Psalm 121 tells us that our help comes from Him. He's the God who made the heaven and the earth. He won't let me stumble, He doesn't sleep, He protects and keeps watch day and night, now and forever.

I'm also glad that Romans 8:28 tells us that all things work together in our life – no matter what they are. God uses the good, the bad and the ugly to work together. Somehow, in His infinite wisdom, He takes some of the difficulties in our life and uses them in a way that brings Him glory.

If we really believe that, then why is it we look to blame the devil when things don't go the way we planned? Or when things go badly? I told some dear friends the other day that we're quick to blame the devil when sometimes we're just dumb and do stupid stuff.

I had that happen to me as I was traveling just last week. It was late at night and I was alone, in a part of the state that was unfamiliar to me. I relied on my GPS. The GPS didn't do me wrong, I just made a turn before I was supposed to. I was trying to get to a hotel. GPS, who I call "Lola," told me to turn left off the highway, onto the next highway. "Lola" then told me to turn left at Hodd Street. It looked like just a short distance, so I took the next left. WRONG turn. I ended up back on the freeway, with no way to get off again for three miles. So I waved goodbye to the hotel that I could see from the freeway.

Three miles later, dear "Lola" told me to make a right on some street I don't remember. Dear sweet "Lola" sent me down a dirt road. Thinking she was smarter than me, and knew a quicker way, I obeyed. It didn't take long and I began to worry. Out in the middle of nothin', dirt road, a woman alone in the car. You know that icky feeling you get in your gut when you think it could be a dangerous scenario?

As I looked down the road – pitch black I might add, there in the middle of this dirt road was a piece of heavy roadwork equipment with a light on. There was nobody around, just this random piece of equipment OUT IN THE MIDDLE OF NOTHING in the dark, late at night. Now this poor pilgrim feels like she's in a science fiction flick. Waiting for something to jump out of the dark and snatch up her car with her and her luggage in it.

Resisting "Lola's" direction, I turned around as quickly as I could. All I wanted to do was to get back to pavement and have a "do over." As I turned around, and started slowly back on the dirt road toward the highway, there it was. Up from the ground, right next to my car, was a white dove. It flew off the ground, up in the air in front of my car.

Very important side note here: doves feed during the day and don't fly at night. They don't want to be a snack for nocturnal animals. But there it was – a white dove. It was a quick reminder to this poor soul that God was right there with me.

Now don't get all freaky about this. I have no weird notion that the white dove was anything but a sign from my Father that He was right there. I was not alone. He knew I was feeling insecure at that moment and just wanted to get to my hotel.

I tell you this account because I hear people all the time blaming the devil for stuff in their life. I refuse to give that old enemy any credit for anything. If I really believe that my God has a plan for me, that He always has watch over me, that I'm never out of His vision and protection, then how could I do anything but trust that truth. That stupid turn that I made got me in the mess I was in. But God never left me. He even used a dove, that DOESN'T FLY AT NIGHT, to show me He was right there.

So one last comment about "Lola": had I listened to her, I wouldn't have had to wave at the hotel on my way past, from the highway going the wrong way. But I also wouldn't have had this awesome testimony to share. Enjoy your day friends. Keep trusting in Him! He has His eye on you, and protects you as you come and as you go. He loves you enough to even make a dove fly at night if there's a good reason for it.

PERSONAL REFLECTION

- What have you done that was dumb, yet saw the hand of God protect you in the midst of it?

- How have you or others fallen into the trap of blaming the enemy, the devil, or whatever you call him?
  - Bottom line is this: spending your time blaming the devil gets us into the blame game and keeps our eyes off Jesus and the truths He wants to teach us.

- What are you facing right now, maybe because of your own doing, that you just need God?

- How will you ask Him to meet you in that place?

28
Tell The Story

The Ganiere family loves to tell stories. We might even each have some variation of the actual facts, giving us a hoot of a time recounting them. We also take tons of pictures, and enjoy the stories that go along with the pictures. Our kids and their families love to sit and look at those pictures, recounting every precious memory, and some very funny stories that those pictures hold. Pictures of weddings, baby dedications, first day of school, sports, band, camping, musicals and on and on and on, even just plain, ordinary meals together.

Some of those stories include loved ones that are no longer with us. This past weekend, when the family was together, one of our sons heard, for the first time, how his grandfather, my Dad, affectionately known as "Bunka," used to do hill climbing on his Harley back in the day. That story brought back memories that I could share with the kids as well.

One of those memories was how I've had conversations with God, while I'm riding my own bike: "God, I don't know if Dad can see me or not. But would you tell him that I love riding. It would make him smile."

The reason we retell stories, is so that the people in the stories are not forgotten. The impact they had on our lives is not forgotten.

In reading Joshua 3 & 4, I was reminded of the fact that God's people, throughout the Bible, built memorials and told stories of the great things God had done. The reason? So they would know that the hand of the Lord is powerful and that they would always reverence the Lord. Read Joshua 3 & 4 at **biblegateway.com** or look it up on **YouVersion** app for your phone, iPad or tablet.

Focus attention on: Joshua 4:21-24 The Voice:
Joshua: Someday your children will ask you, "What do these stones mean?" 22 And you will tell them, "Israel crossed the Jordan here on dry ground." 23 For the Eternal One, your God, dried up the waters of the Jordan until you crossed over (just as He held back the Red Sea for our parents until they crossed) 24 so that everyone on earth would know how powerful the Eternal is and you would reverence your God, the Eternal, forever.

Tell the story! Tell the story so that the people around you will know that the hand of the Lord is powerful and so that you might always reverence your God.

I was challenged this morning. As much as we enjoy family stories do we tell them with the same vigor of how God has shown Himself powerful so that this and

future generations would always reverence Him?
Do I? Do you?

On Sundays, back in "the old days," there were
"testimony nights." I remember well those Sunday nights
that were dedicated to people sharing the goodness of
their God. Testimonies of how God met them at the very
point of their need. How those testimonies grew our faith
and in the journey of life showed us that just as God met
their need, He would certainly meet ours.

I remember well almost daily conversations with others
about those very same things. We were all encouraged
in the faith, through those shared stories.

Have we stopped telling the story? Sometimes we get
so bogged down with life that we don't even SEE what
God is doing. I would challenge you today to begin
asking God to give you eyes to see. Ask Him to give
you ears to hear. Ask Him to reveal His hand in your
life TODAY. Pick up some "stones" just like they did in
Joshua and build a verbal memorial to all that God has
done – and Tell the Story!

You may be the encouragement someone else needs
to hear today. Tell the Story! Listen for the stories of
others. You may very well find the strength, trust or
grace in the midst of your day-to-day journey as well.

I remember one time I was rejoicing about going to hear
someone's testimony. The person I was telling said very
mockingly: "Ah, if you heard one testimony, you heard
them all." **What a horribly sad commentary.** God is
doing things in our lives EVERY day. New things, every
day! Never tire of telling the stories. Never tire of hearing

those stories. God doesn't do cool stuff in our lives just cuz He can. He does them for the same reason He did them back in Joshua 3 and 4. **"...so that everyone on earth would know how powerful the Eternal is and so that you would reverence your God, the Eternal, forever."**

PERSONAL REFLECTION

- On a separate piece of paper, or in your small group, tell of how you came to Christ.

- Tell of a time that God met a need you had and rejoice together over it.

- Tell of a time that you were fearful and God supplied.

- Tell of a time.......

TELL YOUR STORY!
"So that everyone on earth would know how powerful the Eternal is and so that you would reverence your God, the Eternal, forever."

WRITE YOUR STORY!

_____

_____

_____

_____

_____

_____

_____

_____

_____

_____

_____

_____

_____

_____

WRITE YOUR STORY!

_____

_____

_____

_____

_____

_____

_____

_____

_____

_____

_____

_____

_____

_____

29
Freak-out Moments

As is my normal ritual, following my devotion time, I take a peek at social media and emails. One post on Facebook caught my attention: "What is everyone going to do if all hell breaks loose at the end September? According to the Jewish calendar it will be the end of the Shemitah year." After reading some entertaining responses, I posted this: "No matter when the economy crashes we will do what we always do. Trust God."

Why we fret and worry about things that are out of our control is puzzling to me. We do what we know to do. We get to know Him better in His Word, have regular communication with Him (prayer) and when difficulties come, we cry out to Him and do what He says to do. We trust Him.

We recently took our motorcycles to South Dakota and saw some of the most amazing scenery in our country. On one extremely scenic road, Needles Highway, I had a crisis moment. Having to round a hairpin curve going 10 MPH caused me to panic and I did what I usually do when I panic, I let off the throttle. If you know anything about riding, you know that killed the motor. Right there in the middle of the **uphill hairpin curve**. My biggest concern was that someone was going to come from up hill and not see me, and I'd be like a bug smashed on the front of their car.

In my panic, bike in a dead stop, using every muscle in my body to hold my bike up – I cried out to God. Well, more like freaked out to God. **"I can't do this!!!!! I need you to help me. I can't do this. I need your help!!!!"** Immediately, that still small voice said **"Breathe, do what you know to do."** In full freak out mode, I did what I knew to do. Think! Feet on the ground, every ounce of my weight trying to not let my bike roll backwards; right hand on the throttle AND the brake, left hand on the clutch; slowly, very slowly, release the brake, increase the throttle and release the clutch, all at the same time, and I began to move forward. Right up that hill like a boss. I did it!!!!! I did what I knew to do. God's voice telling me to do what I knew to do calmed my freak out and I moved through the crisis.

After we got to the top of that hill, and my blood pressure returned to normal, I did a happy dance and thanked God for the incredible, timely reminder to do what I knew to do.

So, my word to any of you fretting and worrying about anything, including a possible economic collapse: Do what you know to do. Trust God! So often throughout the Word, Jesus tells us to be ready. If you follow the signs of the time, you know Jesus could come at any moment. Be ready! If you don't know Him, take care of business. Open your heart to Him, ask Him to forgive you of your sin, and help you to live for Him.

His Word, the Bible, tells us everything we need to know to trust Him in every day life, and in perilous times. Read that Word. Have daily conversation with Him (prayer). He wants to talk to us too!

As I said at the beginning of this devotion, I start my day with reading some of the Word. I spend time talking to Him – all day having conversation with Him. Preparing, so that when crisis comes, I know what to do. So that when Jesus comes I will be ready. So when life happens and I get in crisis, I can hear His voice and do what He says. Be ready! God be with you friends!

PERSONAL REFLECTION

- What do you tend to do when you "freak out?"

- How has God shown you in the past that He's right there with you and has your back?

- What are you facing now where you need His help?

- In what way will you prepare for the next crisis in your life?

30
Go Time

God help me! It's "Go Time." All is on the line and it's dependent on my ability to walk in faith. Believing that I've prayed, found the path He's laid before me, and I know as good as my knower can know that it's God's time. It is what I affectionately call the "scary-exciting time," or "amazed-afraid time."

I read about such a time with the disciples in Mark 10:32 NIV *"They were on their way up to Jerusalem, with Jesus leading the way, and the disciples were astonished, while those who followed were afraid."* Some versions say "amazed and afraid." Whether you call it "amazed and afraid" or "scary and exciting," it's those times when we know things are changing and it truly is "go time."

I start second guessing myself saying things like "I'm either dumb enough or believing enough to think God can use me." I would choose to fall on the side of "believing enough," but when my eyes are on me, I'm "dumb enough." When I keep my eyes on God,

I'm "believing enough." But there are times when there's an ongoing battle with my own insecurities.

Then I start questioning God about all my frailties. I find myself saying things like: "But God, do you really know who I am? I know me, do YOU know me God? Are you SURE you want ME to do this?" Of course God knows who I am. Of course He knows my weaknesses. Who am I to second-guess God?

Shifting gears a wee bit: I am unashamedly a Wisconsin Green Bay Packer "cheesehead." GO Pack GO! We love our Green Bay Packers. When Aaron Rodgers, Quarterback for the Green Bay Packers was interviewed as he received the MVP trophy in 2015, he was asked how he could sleep the night before the Super Bowl. He went on to say that he slept a full 8 hours. He had done all his preparation the week before, practicing and all that goes with it, and because of it, he had confidence that he had done all there was to do, so he slept. He didn't toss all night with worry. He didn't struggle with fear, rather had confidence that all was well.

In the same way, when God calls us to do a work, we must do all we know to do to prepare. We seek our God in prayer, getting His heart and direction. We find the path that He has laid out for us and we know as good as our knower can know. And now it's "go time." I go forth with confidence that this is His will. I may be a little like the disciples, amazed and afraid. And that's ok. I'm amazed at all God has done and I'm a touch scared because I don't know what's around the corner. But I know that He does. And I'm more than a little OK with that.

We PRAY, READ THE WORD, HEAR FROM HIM, PREPARE AND FINALLY DO. We commit the results to Him and watch God work through a heart that is wholly committed to Him. Confident in His ability through us, it's Go Time friends. Go boldly into all He's called you to today!

PERSONAL REFLECTION

- How have you experienced those "amazed and afraid" times in your life?

- How have you walked through them?

- How can you be better prepared for those amazed and afraid times again? (life is a series of those you know)

- Thank Him that He disciples you on this path and that you can trust Him.

∽∾ 31 ∾∽
Gettin' Me Some Camel Knees

3 John 1-4 NIV *"The elder, To my dear friend Gaius, whom I love in the truth. Dear friend, I pray that you may enjoy good health and that all may go well with you, even as your soul is getting along well. It gave me great joy to have some brothers come and tell about your faithfulness to the truth and how you continue to walk in the truth. I have no greater joy than to hear that my children are walking in the truth."*

As a parent of four children, I can tell you first hand, there is no greater joy than knowing that my kids are doing well. To know that they are walking in the truth, are not lukewarm in their faith, the relationships in their lives are good, their physical health is good, financially they're making it, all is well.

There is great pain in the heart of a parent if there be one that is not doing well, in any of the ways I mentioned, but especially spiritually. As in all families, there are times when all is not well. One or the other is not enjoying good health, they're struggling financially, or their faith is at crisis point. That kind of pain drives a Christian parent to their knees. I used to joke that before my kids were adults, my knees were going to look like "camel knees." Camels are so ridiculously cute. Everything about them is adorable. Except their knees: ugly, bumpy, wearing to the bone, HUGE knees. Now, all of my children are adults, and I still hit my knees for them, their spouses, and especially for my grandchildren. Workin' on those camel knees.

The question rising up within me is this: Do I pray with that same intensity for those that God has placed in my sphere of influence? What about my brothers and sisters in the faith? Do I have such a great love and joy that John speaks of? As the body of Christ, we have a responsibility and are to love each other in such a way that brings a commitment to build "camel knees" for each other. Are my knees showing the signs for them too? What about my neighbors and those whose path I cross?

One of the churches that we were honored to be on pastoral staff had a Christmas musical every year. There was a HUGE camel that we used to call Omar. Omar's job was to carry one of the kings across the platform to the baby Jesus. Omar was adorable. His facial expression as he peered over the congregation was always memorable. The sight of him on that stage brought ooo's and ah's from nearly everyone in the congregation. He was so adorable. They always hoped he would peer across the sanctuary as though he was greeting each one. He never failed to oblige. His knees are far from the quality of his face. They were knobby, skin worn through, and boney, just as one would expect.

My prayer would be this: Father, that I would have some Omar knees. That my knees speak of the hours spent in thanksgiving and prayer for my kids and grandkids, that my knees are true signs of spiritual warfare. The battles are won on our knees friends. What an honor to be able to walk boldly into the throne of grace, and bow on our knees on behalf of our loved ones and friends.

If your knees show no signs of ugly – don't wait any longer. You're missing an enormous blessing of interceding for them all. You will be able to rest in the fact that you don't have to worry, fret or fix the things that are wrong in the lives of those you love. All you need do is work on your "camel knees." God will do the rest. **Hebrews 4:16,** *"Let us then approach God's throne of grace with confidence, so that we may receive mercy and find grace to help us in our time of need."*

PERSONAL REFLECTION

- What is the shape of your knees?

- What kind of wear do they show?

- Who in your life has needs for the grace, mercy and love of God?

- Who in your life needs to know the love of a Savior?

- Who in your life is fighting for either physical or spiritual life?

- What will you do to show your commitment to work on those camel knees?

NOTES

NOTES

NOTES

36958729R00079

Made in the USA
San Bernardino, CA
05 August 2016